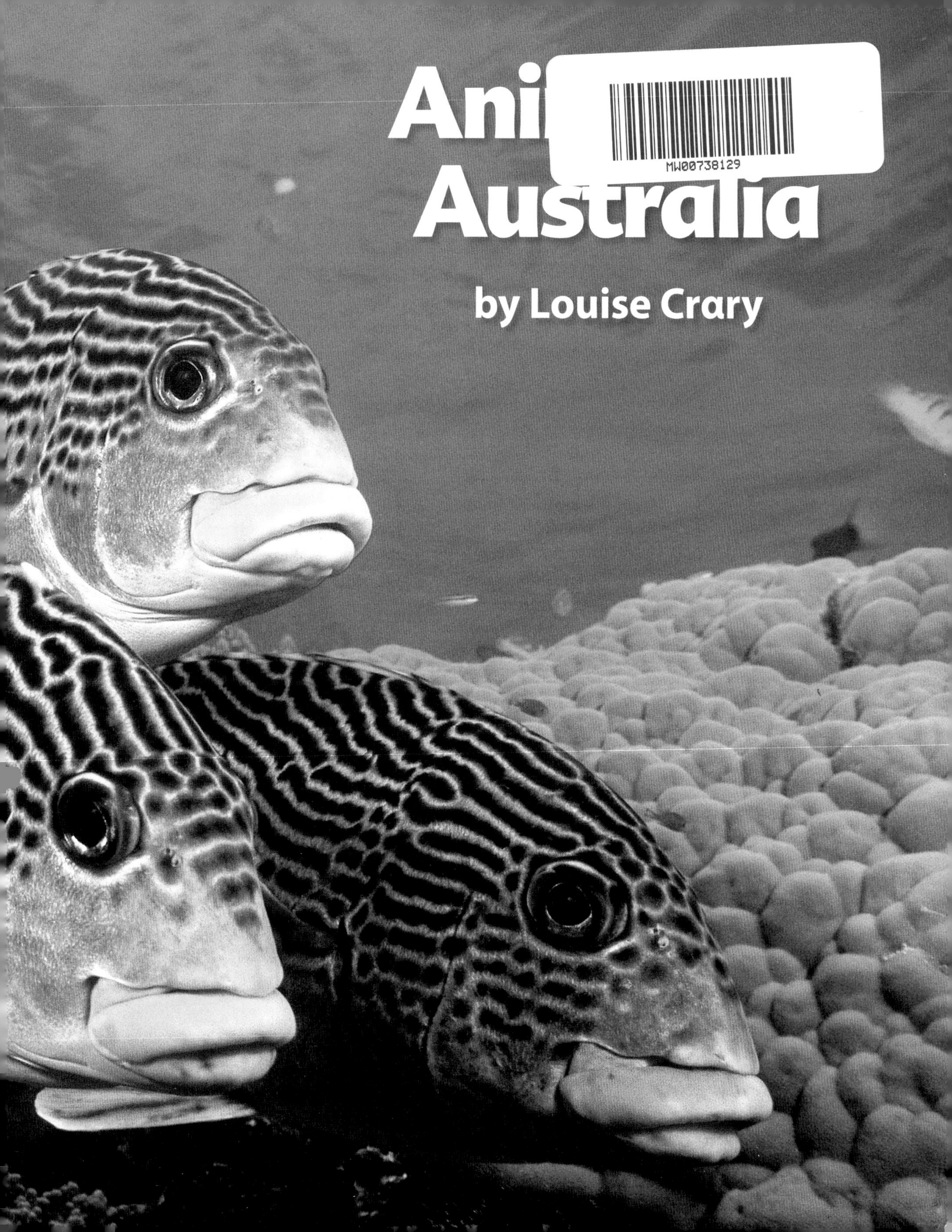

Ani
Australia

by Louise Crary

Many animals live in Australia.

Crocodile

Lorikeet

Dingo

Stingray

Kangaroos live in Australia.

Tails help kangaroos stand.

Emus live in Australia.

Legs help emus run.

Fish live in Australia.

Fins help fish swim.

Koalas live in Australia.

Claws help koalas climb.

Birds live in Australia.

Wings help birds fly.

Sea lions live in Australia.

Fur helps sea lions stay warm.

Animals in Australia